Pi+

THE POSITIVITY INSTITUTE

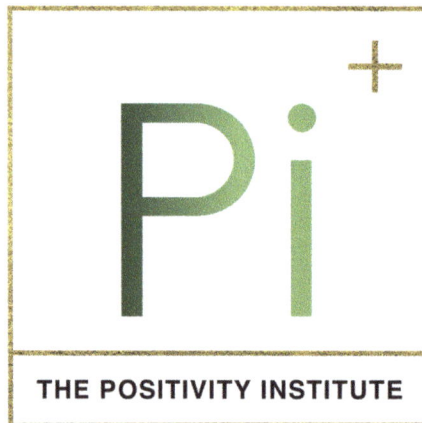

Growing Mentally Tough Teens

Tools for Building Resilience, Achievement and Wellbeing (for 14 to 16 year olds)

STUDENT WORKBOOK

Daniela Falecki and Dr Suzy Green

Acknowledgements

First and foremost, I'd like to give a huge thanks to my colleague and friend Daniela Falecki. Daniela is an awe-inspiring educator who I've been blessed to work with over the years. The creation of the "Growing Mentally Tough Teens" program is the culmination of this very positive relationship and collaboration. In addition, I'd like to thank my own team at PI HQ (The Positivity Institute) who have worked tirelessly through multiple reviews and edits of the program. Finally I'd like to thank our designer, Shauna Haider of We Are Branch in the USA for her creative flair in the design of the program manuals — we love your work! I hope this program not only equips students to better manage the pressure, stress and challenge of school but gives them the mental toughness and strength to create big, hairy, audacious goals that help them create flourishing lives and a flourishing world.

Dr Suzy Green
Clinical & Coaching Psychologist
CEO & Founder of The Positivity Institute

It has been both a privilege and an honour to work with Dr Suzy Green on this project and many others. Her knowledge, wisdom and guidance as a colleague and friend is always valued as I too continue to learn and grow. Of course, nothing would happen if it wasn't for the fabulous PI team who match the 'zestyness' of their inspiring leader. I would also like to acknowledge the numerous teachers who reviewed each draft and shared their feedback to strengthen the program (far too many to mention by name). And let's not forget the students who have already participated in the program and shared their understanding of mental toughness as well as ways they can develop it. As an educator, this is the greatest reward you can have.

Daniela Falecki
Educator
Founder Teacher Wellbeing

About the Authors

Daniela Falecki

B.Ed (Physical Ed & Health), M.Ed (Leadership)

Daniela Falecki, is known as the "keep-it-real" teacher with 25 years experience across primary, secondary and tertiary forms of education in Australia. Having seen first-hand the challenges teachers and schools face in an everchanging landscape, she founded Teacher Wellbeing, which specializes in Positive Psychology interventions to support the development of teacher resilience, wellbeing and collective efficacy. Daniela holds a Masters in Education (Leadership), a Bachelor of Education (HPE), a Certificate in Rudolf Steiner Education, is a licensed Mental Toughness practitioner, and a certified Life Coach and NLP Practitioner. Daniela is a Senior Associate for the Positivity Institute, member of the International Coach Federation, International Positive Psychology Association and lectures at Western Sydney University where she was voted in the top 3 for lecturer of the year for her passionate and engaging style. Daniela currently lives in Sydney, Australia and loves travelling to work with schools on how they can best support their greatest assists, their teachers.

Dr Suzy Green

D.Psyc.(Clin.) MAPS
Founder & CEO, The Positivity Institute

Dr Suzy Green is a Clinical and Coaching Psychologist (MAPS) and Founder & CEO of The Positivity Institute, a positively deviant organisation dedicated to the research and application of Positive Psychology for life, school and work. She is a leader in the complementary fields of Coaching Psychology and Positive Psychology. Suzy was the recipient of an International Positive Psychology Fellowship Award and has published in the Journal of Positive Psychology. She lectured on Applied Positive Psychology as a Senior Adjunct Lecturer in the Coaching Psychology Unit, University of Sydney for ten years and is an Honorary Vice President of the International Society for Coaching Psychology. Suzy also currently holds Honorary Academic positions at the Centre for Positive Psychology, University of Melbourne, the Black Dog Institute and she is an Affiliate of the Institute for Well-Being, Cambridge University. Suzy is an official ambassador for the Starlight Children's Foundation and she maintains a strong media profile appearing on television, radio and in print.

Contents

CONTENTS

Welcome

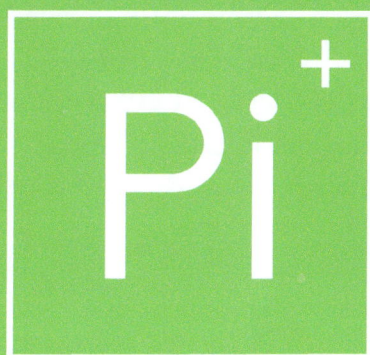

What is Mental Toughness?

Life can be tough at times, especially when you are a teenager at school. Competing demands from parents, teachers and friends … let alone our own self-talk … can sometimes leave us wondering what to do first and how to manage the everyday ups and downs.

This program is here to help.

Mental Toughness is a term you typically hear in sports psychology to explain the skills of how successful people manage the pressure of competition, the pressure from their own expectations and the stress that comes from failures and setbacks.

You see, success is not something we are just born with; it requires trial and error, reflection, practice and so much more. But I know you already know this. Perhaps what you don't know is that new developments in science can help us narrow down the specific cognitive, social and emotional skills that athletes have been using for years — to help us better navigate school and life in general.

- Imagine you were able to feel in control of your own life and outcomes

- Imagine you had specific tools to help you achieve more but in less time

- Imagine you got to choose what challenges you wanted to take on

- Imagine you felt confident enough to speak up in front of your peers when you wanted to

- These are all skills of mentally tough people.

Mental toughness is not about being macho; it's about being wise. It's not about competing with others but acknowledging our unique strengths and differences. It's not about working harder but working smarter, in the right way at the right time. At the end of the day we're not at school just to learn content for exams — we are here to learn about our potential, we need the skills to manage the pressure of learning and we would do well to acknowledge the world of possibility that lies ahead of us.

About the Program

Pi⁺

About Mentally Tough Teens

Mental Toughness is a personality trait which determines, in large part, how people respond to challenge, stress and pressure … irrespective of their circumstances (Clough & Strycharczyk, 2012). To better understand the concepts surrounding mental toughness, researchers have developed a framework they call the 4Cs of Mental Toughness.

This program has been designed to help you understand and develop skills within the 4Cs so you can better navigate the daily stressors, challenges and pressures that you face now and may face in the future. The four key questions that relate to the Model of Mental Toughness and will be explored in this program are:

Control:
How well do you believe you control your own destiny?

Commitment:
How well do you stick to tasks?

Challenge:
How well do you seek challenges as a way of learning?

Confidence:
How well do you speak with confidence and work with others?

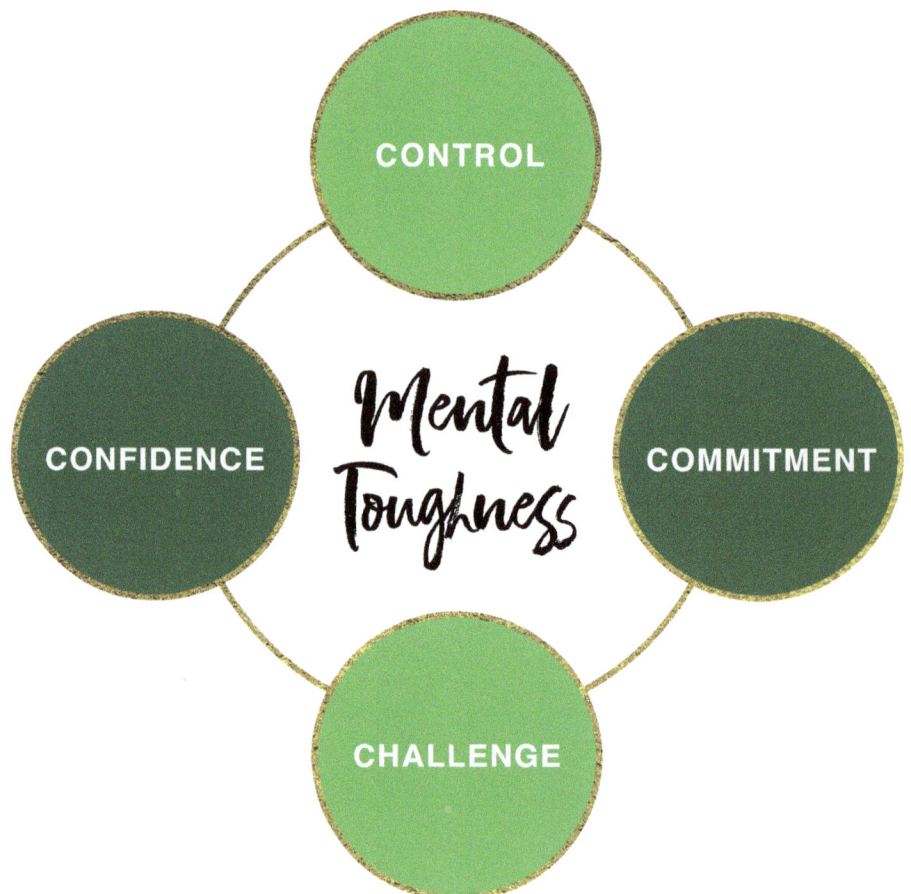

Unit 1

Toughening Up
(The What and Why
of Mental Toughness)

Pi⁺

Unit 1

Purpose of this unit

The purpose of this unit is to provide an overview of the program including that of the 4Cs of Mental Toughness — Control, Commitment, Challenge and Confidence.

Mental Toughness is necessary in order for us to be resilient during times of stress, pressure and challenge. Stress is a normal part of our life; however if not managed effectively it can be detrimental to our wellbeing and impact our levels of achievement. Learning to be brave, courageous and resilient (when learning) may be a skill you have heard of before ... but now we want to take this to the next level with specific skills that develop our Mental Toughness.

Lesson 1

Purpose

This session is designed to:

- Introduce the program and explore expectations

- Define Mental Toughness

- Explain the 4Cs model of Mental Toughness

- Measure Mental Toughness

1.1.1 — Defining Mental Toughness

1. Mental Toughness is …

_____

_____

_____

_____

2. What are some challenges you have experienced? E.g. arguments with parents or friends, managing school work, moving house, etc.

_____

_____

_____

_____

3. How did you respond to these challenges? E.g. got angry, avoided, blamed, faced them head-on etc.

_____

_____

_____

_____

1.1.2 Measuring Mental Toughness Survey

Understanding the 4Cs	Self-rating scale: Circle where you think you currently lie
Control (Life) The Control-life scale refers to how much control you believe you have in your life. Do you believe you have complete control over everything in your life (10/10), or do you believe you are at the mercy of everything around you (1/10)?	1 2 3 4 5 6 7 8 9 10
Control (Emotions) The Control-emotions scale refers to how well you are able to manage your emotions. Are you able to completely control your emotions to a point of shutting off (10/10), or do your emotions control you to a point where you find it difficult to function (1/10)?	1 2 3 4 5 6 7 8 9 10
Commitment (Setting Goals) This Commitment scale refers to how often and how well you set goals for yourself. Do you set goals, create a vision or set an intention for how you want learning or tasks to be (10/10), or do you let others tell you what to do and how you should be when it comes to learning and achieving (1/10)?	1 2 3 4 5 6 7 8 9 10
Commitment (Achieving Goals) This Commitment scale refers to the way in which you work towards your goals and targets. Do you keep the promises you make to yourself and others when it comes to achieving tasks or goals (10/10), or do you often make promises to yourself and others and not follow through or achieve them (1/10)?	1 2 3 4 5 6 7 8 9 10

Challenge (Take on Challenges) This Challenge scale refers to how you see new opportunities, challenges and change. Do you seek out and embrace challenges as opportunities for growth and learning (10/10), or do you avoid challenges, preferring to stay inside your comfort zone (1/10)?	1 2 3 4 5 6 7 8 9 10
Challenge (Overcome Challenges) This Challenge scale refers to how you overcome challenges and change. Do you reflect on mistakes or failures as opportunities for growth and learning and try again (10/10), or do you reflect on mistake and failures as just the way it is and accept the result (1/10)?	1 2 3 4 5 6 7 8 9 10
Confidence (Abilities) The Confidence-abilities scale refers to your awareness and use of your strengths. Do you confidently know and use your strengths when needed (10/10), or are you uncertain about your strengths and your own abilities when it comes to learning (1/10)?	1 2 3 4 5 6 7 8 9 10
Confidence (Relationships) This Commitment scale refers to the way The Confidence-relationships scale refers to how assertive, reliable and supportive you are in relationships. Do you stand your ground in a respectful manner when you're expressing your point or view (10/10), or do you become intimidated and easily led by others' opinions, preferring to hide in the background (1/10)?	1 2 3 4 5 6 7 8 9 10

4. Discuss with a partner why you chose the scores you did...

_____

_____

_____

1.1.3 — Can you develop Mental Toughness?

Mental Toughness is a term you typically hear in sports psychology to explain the skills of how successful people manage the pressure of competition, the pressure from their own expectations and the stress that comes from failures and setbacks.

Success is not something we are just born with; it requires trial and error, reflection, practice and so much more — but I know you already know this. Perhaps what you don't know is that new developments in science can help us narrow down the specific cognitive, social and emotional skills that athletes have been using for years, to help us better navigate school and life in general.

The four key questions that relate to the Model of Mental Toughness and will be explored in this program are:

1. Control: How well do you believe you control your own destiny?

2. Commitment: How well do you stick to tasks?

3. Challenge: How well do you seek challenges as a way of learning?

4. Confidence: How well do you speak with confidence and work with others?

CONTROL

Mental Toughness

CONFIDENCE

COMMITMENT

CHALLENGE

Looking at the 4Cs, which of these four do you think you do well and which one do you think you could develop more? The area where I do well (with an example) is:

_____

_____

_____

The area where I could improve (with an example) is:

_____

_____

_____

_____

Lesson 2

Purpose

This session is designed to:

- The nature and causes of stress

- How stress affects the body

- The impact of ongoing stress on wellbeing

- Healthy ways to manage stress

1.2.1 — Pressure Points

We all experience stress differently with each of us having our own pressure points. These are the points where we have a stress response either physically in our body or in our mind. Use the table below to make a list of your own personal stress pressure points.

Event or situation	From your perspective, what causes this stress?	From your perspective, what causes this stress?
E.g. Arguing with parents	They don't listen to me	I hide in my room

1.2.2 — A Bunny's Challenge

Can you help the rabbit get to his eggs? Ready, set, go!

Questions

1. How did you respond to the pressure?

2. What were you thinking and feeling?

1.2.3 — Video Reflection

1.2.4 — My MEDS Journal

We all experience stress in varying degrees at various times. There are however some basic things we can do to support ourselves through stressful times. These include taking our MEDS (Meditation, Exercise, Diet and Sleep). Use the table below to track how often you are taking your MEDS to support your wellbeing:

MEDS	Meditation	Exercise	Diet	Sleep
	What activity did you do? For how long?	What activity did you do? For how long?	How balanced was your nutrition today? Give examples.	How well did you sleep last night? Explain.
Day 1				
Day 2				
Day 3				
Day 4				
Day 5				
Day 6				
Day 7				

Overall Reflection

_____

_____

Lesson 3

Purpose

This session is designed to:

- Explore the decisions we make to support our own wellbeing

- Identify helpful and harmful coping strategies for stress

- Recognise safe and reliable places to access further support

1.3.1 — My MEDS Bingo

Walk around the room and find one person who meets the criteria for each of the squares in the grid. These activities are related to your MEDS Journal that you completed. If someone has done an activity in the past week, they can then sign their name in the relevant square. Each student can sign their name a maximum of twice. Once you have a signature in all squares, you call out BINGO!

Practiced three meditations	Participated in a sport	Consistently had a healthy breakfast	Slept eight hours consistently
Went to bed before 9.00pm one night	Ate vegetables every day	Went to the gym	Practiced mindful breathing
Went for a walk in nature	Practiced a mindfulness activity	Used music or an app to fall asleep	Limited their sugar intake
Loved the comfort of their bed	Ate three lunches through the week	Did exercise with friends	Prefers to exercise in the afternoon rather than the morning
Drank two litres of water per day	Made their own dinner	Used a mindfulness app	Found it easy to wake up in the morning

1.3.2 — Coping Strategies (Part 1)

We all cope differently with different challenges. Most of our coping strategies are learned behaviours from watching others; however as we get older we can more consciously learn new ways to better cope with challenges. Have a look at the list below and put a circle around five positive coping strategies and a line through five negative coping strategies:

Eat too much	Talk to someone	Sleep too much	Blame yourself
Meditate	Not eat at all	Worry endlessly	Think about possibilities
Consume high sugar drinks e.g. Red Bull	Go for a walk	Blame other people	Daydream
Rant on Facebook	Join a safe online chat club e.g. ReachOut.com	Learn (and read) from experts	Write a plan of what to do
Play a sport	Give up	Access my competitive streak	Sit in nature
Criticise self	Pick a fight with someone	Set a goal to move forward	Avoid doing a task
Get angry and start a fight	Seek support from others	Sit and watch Netflix	Drink tea or coffee
Try harder	Listen to music to calm down	Organise my time	Talk things through with someone
Pretend something doesn't exist	Play computer games	Punch a pillow	Write in a journal
Phone a friend	Practice deep breathing	Take action to get something done	Paint or draw

1.3.3 — Coping Strategies (Part 2)

When we have specific helpful coping strategies we become more resilient to stress. Resilience is our ability to adapt to risks and adversity. It relates to how well we bounce back from challenges.

Mental toughness is about consciously choosing measured risks to grow, to accept and manage challenges for the purpose of improvement and satisfaction.

To do this we must acknowledge stress and focus on the areas of our life we can control (instead of the areas we can't control). By doing so we are more likely to stay focused and motivated for peak performance.

This can be seen in the stress curve below:

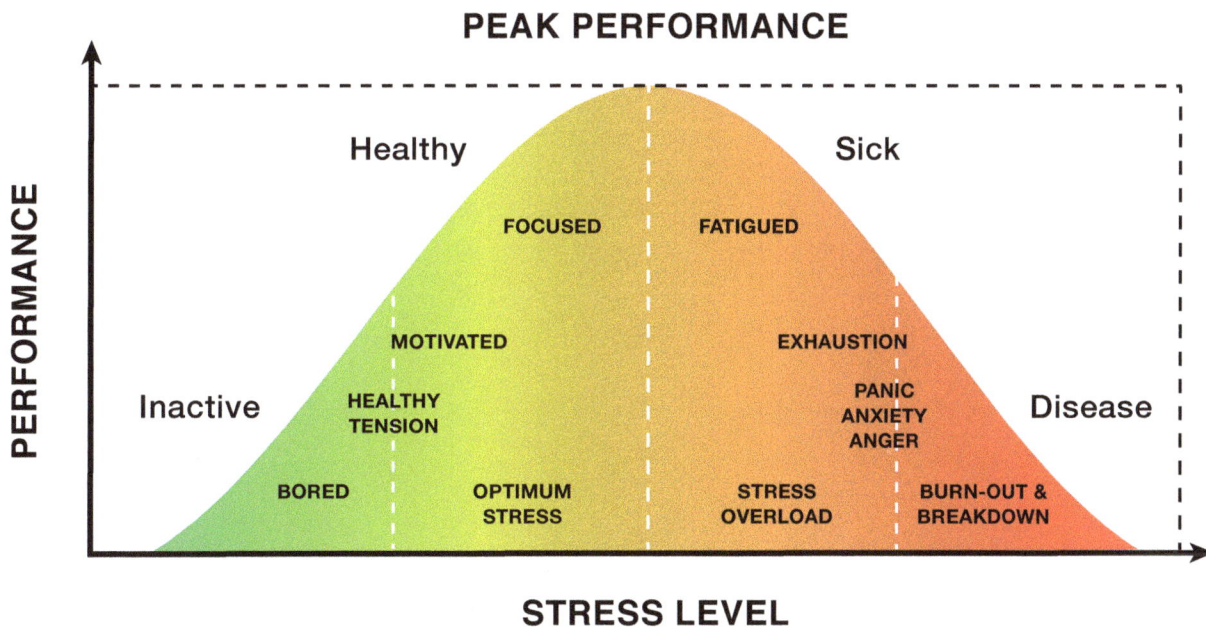

PEAK PERFORMANCE

Healthy · Sick

FOCUSED · FATIGUED

MOTIVATED · EXHAUSTION

Inactive · HEALTHY TENSION · PANIC ANXIETY ANGER · Disease

BORED · OPTIMUM STRESS · STRESS OVERLOAD · BURN-OUT & BREAKDOWN

PERFORMANCE

STRESS LEVEL

Now it's your turn...

1. Think of a time when you have been bored and unmotivated when doing an activity. What caused this feeling? How did this affect your performance?

_____

_____

_____

_____

_____

2. Think of a time when you have been fatigued and overloaded. What caused this feeling? How did this affect your performance?

_____

_____

_____

_____

_____

1.3.4 — Coping Strategies (Part 3)

Earlier in the unit, we identified some pressure points or situations where we may experience stress. Use the table below to identify both helpful and harmful ways of coping with these situations. Examples of situations could be disagreements with friends, pressure from parents, worries about exams, etc. Complete the first one then add your own.

Challenges	Helpful coping strategies	Harmful coping strategies
1. Feeling tired and grumpy		

What about when it all gets too tough? Remember you are not alone; there are many great resources and support networks available. The most important thing is that if you (or a friend) need extra help, be sure to ask for it.

Here are some great resources you can access any time:

• ReachOut.com — http://au.reachout.com

• Youth Beyond Blue — http://www.youthbeyondblue.com

• Bite Back (Blackdog Institute) — https://www.biteback.org.au

• Kids Help Line — https://kidshelpline.com.au

1.3.5 — Toughening Up

In this unit, we have explored the concept of mental toughness and the 4Cs of Control, Commitment, Challenge and Confidence. But in order to be mentally tough, we also need to acknowledge stress and how we can best manage this. Only when we are able to better manage everyday stresses can we move beyond surviving ... to thriving and peak performance.

We have also identified that in order to grow and learn, stress is a normal part of the process. Having helpful ways to manage stress can make us more resilient to the everyday demands that exist in life.

The next step for you is to put all this together by thinking of an upcoming challenge you may have ahead of you ... e.g. a term test, an assignment, a music recital, a debate, a sporting event, etc. Think about how could you stretch yourself to grow and improve. How can you plan specific coping strategies that are helpful and could support you during this challenge?

What is an upcoming challenge for you?	What do you already do well?	How could you stretch yourself to improve?	What helpful coping strategies will you use?

Unit 2

Becoming Captain of Your Destiny (Life Control)

Pi+

Unit 2

Purpose of this unit

The purpose of this unit is to explore the concept of 'Life Control'. Control is the extent to which you feel you are in control of your life and that you can make a difference and change things — whether you feel you have control over the events that happen in your life or whether you think you are at the mercy of everyone around you because you have no control over what happens.

By developing an understanding of the areas where we do have control over our life, and the areas where we don't, we become mentally tough and more resilient to life's challenges.

Lesson 4

Purpose

This session is designed to:

- Identify the differences between **Internal Locus of Control** and **External Locus of Control**

- Explore the areas in life we are concerned about but can't control

- Provide examples of how we as individuals can influence aspects of our lives

2.4.1 — Locus of Control

A person's Locus of Control is the belief of how much control they feel they have over the circumstances that occur in their life. That is, do you believe the big things in your life are controlled by yourself or by external forces such as fate, luck, God, or teachers and parents?

A person with an External Locus of Control believes their life is guided by fate, luck or other external circumstances … such as other people and other events. A person with an Internal Locus of Control believes their life is guided by their own personal decisions and efforts.

In general, those people who have an internal locus of control tend to be more mentally tough and capable of influencing what happens in their lives.

Have you ever done something and thought to yourself you were 'really lucky' to win or to get a good grade on an assignment? This is an example of an external locus of control. Or, did you think to yourself: 'I worked really hard and deserved the good result'? This is an example of an internal locus of control. Try to think of some more examples …

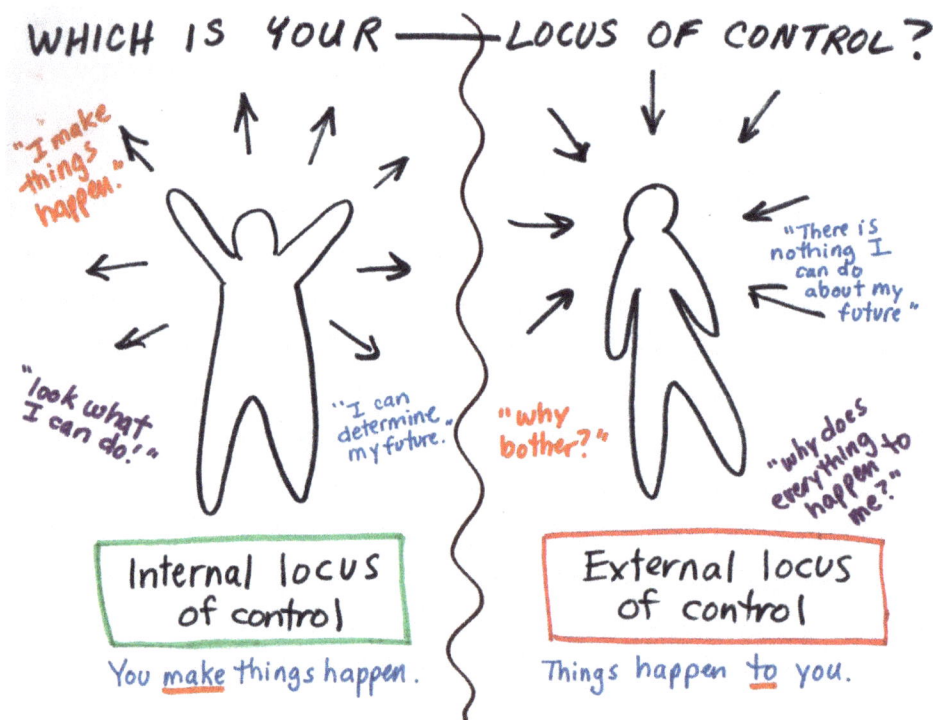

Source: http://overcoming-depression.org/locusofcontrol/

WHICH IS YOUR ——→ LOCUS OF CONTROL?

"I make things happen."

"look what I can do!"

"I can determine my future."

Internal locus of control

You **make** things happen.

"There is nothing I can do about my future"

"why bother?"

"why does everything to happen to me?"

External locus of control

Things happen **to** you.

Examples of an External Locus of Control:

_____

_____

_____

_____

_____

Examples of an Internal Locus of Control:

_____

_____

_____

_____

_____

2.4.2 — Circle of Concern and Circle of Influence

Adapted from The Seven Habits of Highly Effective People by Stephen R. Covey, Simon & Schuster (1992). There are many things that happen in our lives that we can control and may aspects we can't control. For example, we can control if we decide to do our homework, but we can't control if the teacher will check it or not. We can control deciding to invite a friend to the movies but we can't control if they are going to come or not.

A person's Circle of Concern involves a wide range of concerns such as our health, our friends, problems at school, the nature of a school system and its policies. A person's Circle of Influence involves those concerns where we can do something about them. They are the concerns we have some control over. The purpose here is to be proactive in our lives instead of reactive. Stephen Covey defines proactive as 'being responsible for our own lives … our behaviour is a function of our decisions, not our conditions'. This means proactive people focus on issues within their circle of influence. They work on things they can do something about. Doing so increases their Circle of Influence. Reactive people tend to blame others and prefer to whinge rather than be proactive in addressing issues they are concerned about.

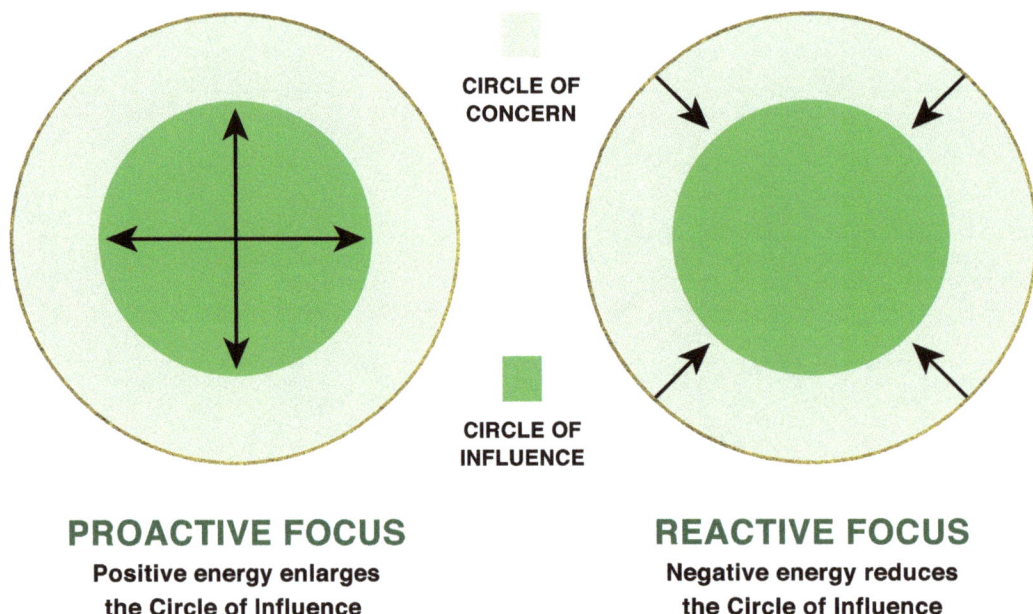

CIRCLE OF CONCERN

CIRCLE OF INFLUENCE

PROACTIVE FOCUS
Positive energy enlarges the Circle of Influence

REACTIVE FOCUS
Negative energy reduces the Circle of Influence

Adapted from the Centre For Confidence:
http://www.centreforconfidence.co.uk/pp/techniques.php?p=c2lkPTYmdGlkPTMmaWQ9MzU

Now it's your turn...

Brainstorm all the areas in your life that are a concern to you — e.g. world peace, famine, school grades, career planning, family pressure, etc.

Then write down all the areas of these concerns that you can control.

Write these in the next worksheet and share with a partner to uncover any similarities or differences.

Stephen R. Covey's 'Seven Habits of Highly Effective People' discusses the power of perception when choosing to be either re-active or pro-active. He does this by defining the areas in our life that we can control and the areas we cannot control.

Write, in the centre circle, all the things at school you have control over. Write all the things you are concerned about but have no control over in the outer circle.

CIRCLE OF CONCERN

Areas where you have no control

CIRCLE OF INFLUENCE

Areas you can control

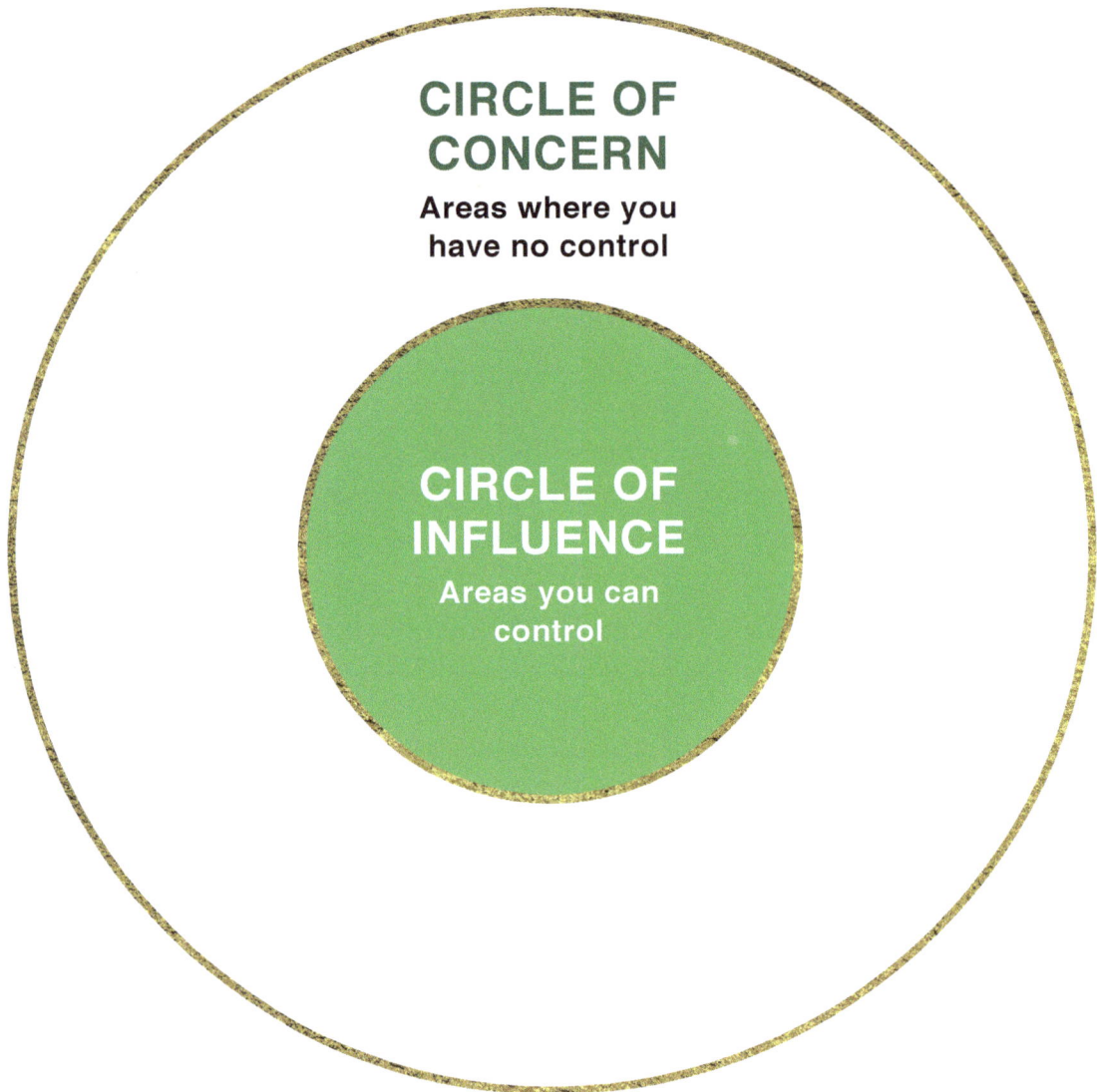

What is the biggest difference between the areas you can and can't control?

2.4.3 — My Take-aways about CONTROL

What are the three biggest insights, learnings and strategies you have taken away from this lesson?

1. _____

   _____

2. _____

   _____

3. _____

   _____

Lesson 5

Purpose

This session is designed to:

- Build an understanding of Learned Optimism and Learned Helplessness

- Explore explanatory styles and how they impact our decisions and behaviours

- Link explanatory styles to ANTS and PETS

2.5.1 — Learned Optimism versus Learned Helplessness

Learned Optimism is:

_____

_____

_____

_____

Learned Helplessness is:

_____

_____

_____

_____

Explanatory Styles

Martin Seligman described explanatory style as 'the manner in which you habitually explain to yourself why events happen' (Seligman, 1990).

That is, the little stories we tell ourselves to make sense of our life.

You may have heard of ANTS (Automatic Negative Thoughts) and PETS (Performance Enhancing Thoughts) before? That's the automatic voices in your head telling you can or can't do something. Your explanatory style is the next step to better understanding these and it helps us identify if we are being more pessimistic or optimistic. To do this we need to use the 3Ps.

Personalisation

This relates to what you believe is the cause of something, e.g. imagine you lost a game of tennis.

- A pessimist will interpret the cause as personal ('I failed').

- An optimist allows for non-personal factors ('Grass just isn't my surface').

Permanence

This relates to the perception of time, e.g. do you perceive a result as permanent or temporary?

- A pessimist will interpret setbacks as permanent ('I'll never get better at this subject').

- An optimist sees the setback as temporary ('I didn't prepare well this time; I should have studied more').

Pervasiveness

This relates to the perception of space, e.g. do you perceive that if you did poorly in one area that this means you will do poorly in every area?

- A pessimist will see setbacks as all-pervasive ('Nothing works out for me').

- An optimist will see the setback as specific to one area of life ('At least I did well in other areas').

2.5.2 — Case Study

Consider two people, Gabby and Fatima, who are both applying for the same part-time job. Both of them are unsuccessful.

Gabby is a pessimist. She assumes, rightly or wrongly, that the reason she missed out is personal (I wasn't good enough), and/or permanent (I'll never get a job), and/or pervasive (this ruins everything). With this explanatory style Gabby is at risk of giving up on herself, is less likely to try again and is also more vulnerable to spiralling into poor mental health.

In contrast, Fatima is an optimist. Faced with the identical setback she assumes the cause is non-personal (someone else was obviously more suitable), and temporary (there are other jobs I can apply for), and non-pervasive (at least it doesn't impact my school and sporting commitments).

Now it's your turn … Think of a setback you have faced in the past year.

1. How might a pessimist respond and think?

_____

_____

_____

_____

2. How might an optimist respond and think?

_____

_____

_____

_____

2.5.3 — My Take-aways about CONTROL

What are the three biggest insights, learnings and strategies you have taken away from this lesson?

1. _____

_____

2. _____

_____

3. _____

_____

Lesson 6

Purpose

This session is designed to:

- Explore the impact of distractions on our ability to focus

- Practice ways to focus our attention

- Plan for ways to limit distractions

2.6.1 — Number Grids

Below is a number grid. Your task is to indicate (point to) with a pen — but do not mark — the sequence of numbers beginning at 0. You have 90 seconds to see how many consecutive numbers you can find.

Version 1

24	43	58	90	49	67	89	86	62	50
3	64	76	84	10	52	27	94	8	77
92	45	53	37	29	17	54	42	19	99
81	00	22	57	31	96	39	12	33	20
25	36	65	88	14	2	78	85	47	87
56	13	6	74	48	23	90	73	98	91
60	41	80	5	11	51	68	38	72	83
97	75	34	79	26	46	82	9	63	16
35	44	21	40	1	69	61	7	55	71
4	30	93	66	59	32	18	70	28	15

Version 2

00	16	53	29	58	31	7	15	38	6
24	54	59	87	2	72	46	48	28	27
42	10	63	37	65	90	14	88	62	74
35	67	71	34	13	3	64	73	5	91
52	25	80	1	45	21	51	20	75	39
43	70	84	89	50	30	81	33	49	98
17	36	60	12	57	94	19	95	83	4
11	61	92	44	78	22	55	85	99	56
66	9	23	93	8	69	77	32	96	97
26	68	79	86	18	41	47	82	76	40

2.6.2 — My Take-aways about CONTROL

What are the three biggest insights, learnings and strategies you have taken away from this lesson?

1. _____

_____

2. _____

_____

3. _____

_____

Unit 3

Riding the emotional rollercoaster (Emotional Control)

Pi+

Unit 3

Purpose of this unit

The purpose of this unit is to explore the concept of 'Emotional Control'. Emotional Control is the extent to which you feel you are able to control your emotions; as well as being aware of the emotions of others.

If you are high on Emotional Control you are better able to control your emotions … meaning you are able to keep your anxieties in check and are less likely to be distracted by the emotions of others or reveal your emotional state to other people. Alternatively, if you are at the other end of the scale and low on emotional control, you may be driven by your emotions and therefore be more reactive to events around you (instead of proactive).

Lesson 7

Purpose

This session is designed to:

- Build emotional literacy

- Map emotions along a continuum through a day

- Explore how we manage emotions

3.7.1 — Word Bank of Emotions

Thrilled	Cherish	Proud	Respect
Cheerful	Thankful	Wonderful	Bitter
Fantastic	Marvellous	Amazed	Miserable
Awful	Devoted	Embarrassed	Exhuberant
Determined	Despair	Exposed	Frightened
Relieved	Loved	Focused	Isolated
Trusting	Gloomy	Regretful	Grateful
Ashamed	Surprised	Powerful	Serene
Regretful	Terrified	Shy	Confident
Elated	Playful	Excluded	Humorous
Attentive	Puzzled	Engaged	Bothered
Crushed	Compassionate	Caring	Confident
Hopeful	Irritated	Humiliated	Optimistic

3.7.2 – Mapping Emotions

Think about your day yesterday at school, or the last day you were at school. As you reflect on this day, map your feelings from hour to hour by placing a cross on the scale below. You may like to use the scale of emotions you just created as a rough guide.

Once you have mapped your emotions, draw a line through them to see how your emotions moved throughout the day. Share your findings with a partner.

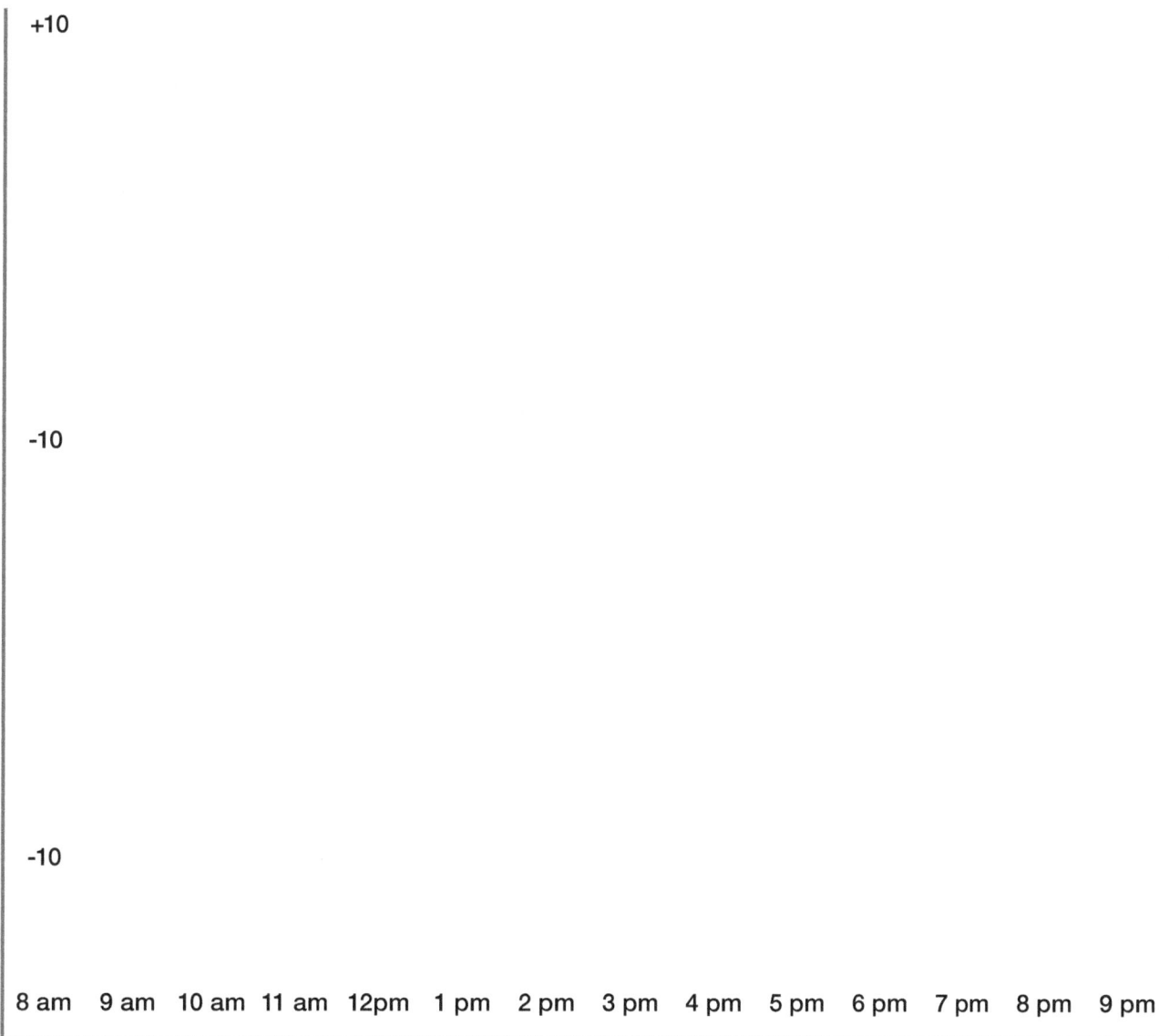

+10

-10

-10

8 am   9 am   10 am   11 am   12pm   1 pm   2 pm   3 pm   4 pm   5 pm   6 pm   7 pm   8 pm   9 pm

3.7.3 — Understanding Emotions

Complete the following statements:

I become frustrated when:

_____

_____

_____

I get scared when:

_____

_____

_____

I am proud of myself when:

_____

_____

_____

I am focused when:

_____

_____

_____

How do you manage emotions?

Look at the list of emotions and draw a line to the strategy you use to manage this emotion. You can draw a line to the same strategy more than once and you can even add your own strategy if it does not appear here.

Angry	Exercise or play a sport
	Punch a pillow
Sad	Listen to music
	Go for a walk
Excited	Paint, write or draw
	Verbally lash out at others
Thankful	Blame parents or teachers
	Ask for support from others
	Talk to friends
Proud	Be kind to myself
	Have a good cry
Hurt	Breathe deeply
	Turn to food and snacks
Anxious	Ignore it and pretend it doesn't exist
	Become competitive and work harder
Determined	Other …

Share with a partner what you uncovered about how you manage emotions.

3.7.4 — My Take-aways about CONTROL

What are the three biggest insights, learnings and strategies you have taken away from this lesson?

1. _____

_____

2. _____

_____

3. _____

_____

Lesson 8

Purpose

This session is designed to:

- Increase understanding of the thought-feeling loop

- Practice ways to manage anxiety

- Explore the relationship between thoughts and heart rate

- Demonstrate relaxation techniques

3.8.1 — Thought-Feeling-Behaviour Loop

Complete the table below to identify how someone might be feeling, and their behaviour when they have certain thoughts.

Situation	Thoughts	Feelings	Behaviour
You just found out your best friend went to the movies without you	Positive Thought Negative Thought		
You have an exam tomorrow	Positive Thought Negative Thought		
You received your assignment back from a teacher with a poor grade	Positive Thought Negative Thought		
Your parents asked you to babysit tonight when they know you have a friend's birthday party	Positive Thought Negative Thought		

3.8.2 — Heart–Rhythm Patterns

The HeartMath Institute has been doing research for years on the relationship between our thoughts and the impact on our physiology; more specifically, the heart. This research has shown how our breaths and thoughts can directly influence the rhythms of our heart.

When we experience stress, frustration and anxiety, our heart rate becomes erratic and sharp; whereas when we experience appreciation and gratitude, our heart moves into what scientists call 'a coherent state'.

Heart-Rhythm **Patterns**

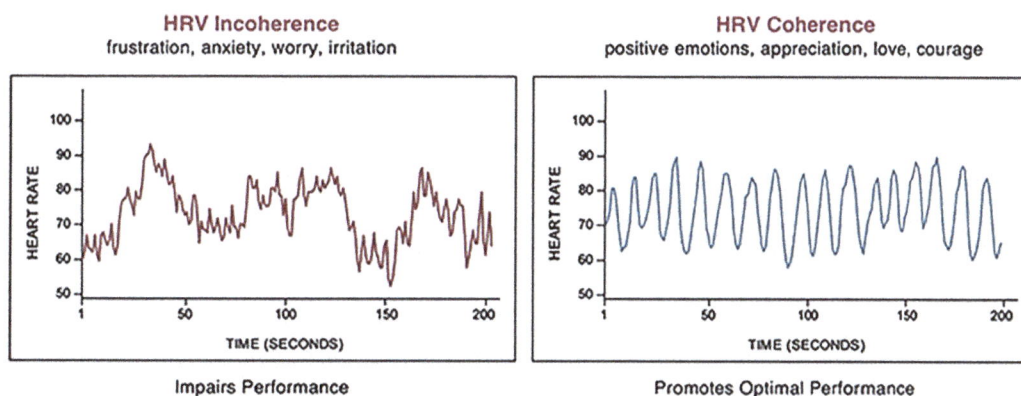

Sourced from Heartmath: *https://www.heartmath.org/articles-of-the-heart/study-looks-coherence-feeling-states/*

Now it's your turn …

Close your eyes and think about something that is stressful or challenging and notice any sensations in your body such as your breath, shoulders, stomach area, or anywhere else in your body. How did your body respond when you had these thoughts?

Now practice coherent breathing using the instructions on the next page. You can increase your coherence in about a minute, practicing the simple quick steps of this technique. It is especially useful when you begin feeling a draining emotion or negative emotional states such as frustration, irritation or anxiety.

- **Step 1:** Heart-Focused breathing. Focus your attention in the area of the heart. Imagine your breath is flowing in and out of your heart or chest area, breathing a little slower and deeper than usual. Suggestion: Inhale five seconds, exhale five seconds (or whatever rhythm is comfortable).

- **Step 2:** Activate a Positive Feeling. Make a sincere attempt to experience a regenerative feeling such as appreciation or care for someone or something in your life. Suggestion: Try to re-experience the feeling you have for someone you love, a pet, a special place, an accomplishment, etc … or focus on a feeling of calm or ease.

Questions

1. What was easy or hard for you?

_____

_____

_____

2. Did you notice or feel any changes in your heart rhythm?

_____

_____

_____

3. How could you use coherent breathing in the future?

_____

_____

_____

3.8.3 — My Take-aways about CONTROL

What are the three biggest insights, learnings and strategies you have taken away from this lesson?

1. _____

_____

2. _____

_____

3. _____

_____

Lesson 9

Purpose

This session is designed to:

- Increase students' positive emotions

- Experience the power of laughter as a tool for emotional management

- Practice Optimistic Thinking with the ABCDE technique

3.9.1 — Practicing Optimistic Thinking

Now that we've explored in detail the relationship with thoughts and feelings, we explain how we can influence these thoughts to move towards a more optimistic perspective. The point here is that by being actively aware of our thoughts, we become actively aware of our emotions.

Optimism is described as looking on the bright side, of thinking and feeling that events will be positive; while pessimism is looking at the dark side of a situation and highlighting what did (or will) go wrong.

Given optimistic thinking has a positive impact on our emotions and can alleviate anxiety, it is important to have strategies to support optimism. The ABCDE technique is one way we can question our ANTS and reframe them to PETS.

A is the adversity — the event that triggers stress or worry. E.g. challenges within a friendship, a speech you have to give in class, an exam or performance.

B is the belief — this is the thought you have and how you interpret the adversity. E.g. a person about to give a speech for an assessment task may think, "I'm not good at talking in front of others," or "Other people do it so much better than me."

C is for consequences — what could happen or did happen as a result of these beliefs? E.g. the repetitious thinking or saying to yourself you are not good at giving speeches is called rumination. This can be debilitating and result in you stuttering, reading notes and not delivering your true knowledge.

D is for disputing the thought — this means questioning if the belief is really true. It means gathering evidence to identify if a belief is valid or not. This is a bit like arguing with yourself to recognise that there is another way to think and see the outcome. E.g. a person gives really good speeches when in front of friends or family — so saying they are not good at giving speeches is incorrect.

E is for energy — this means checking in with your emotions to see how it feels when you have a new thought.

Here is an example:

A Adversity	B Belief	C Consequences	D Disputing the thought	E Energy
Think of a recent challenge you would like to improve upon … what happened? What was the challenge?	What thoughts did you have when this event occurred? What do you think about this now?	What were the consequences of these thoughts? How did it feel? What did you do?	Is this thought/belief really true? How do you know? What evidence do you have to prove or disprove this belief?	If you were going to look at this differently, what might be a new perspective? How does this perspective feel? How could you action this new belief? What might be the consequences of this action?
Example: "I didn't get the score I wanted or expected in my assessment tasks."	**Example:** "I was disappointed because I tried really hard and I thought my teacher didn't explain it properly."	**Example:** "I feel angry at my teacher for not being clear and sometimes think, 'why should I try so hard when it doesn't matter'?"	**Example:** "My teacher often says to ask them for help if I need it. My teacher also did provide an example with resources for us to use."	**Example:** "While my teacher could've explained it better, I could've asked more questions, searched for more resources and shown them a draft. This assessment result is only part of the whole and I can get more support next time."

Now it's your turn...

A Adversity	B Belief	C Consequences	D Disputing the thought	E Energy
Think of a recent challenge you would like to improve upon … what happened? What was the challenge?	What thoughts did you have when this event occurred? What do you think about this now?	What were the consequences of these thoughts? How did it feel? What did you do?	Is this thought/belief really true? How do you know? What evidence do you have to prove or disprove this belief?	If you were going to look at this differently, what might be a new perspective? How does this perspective feel? How could you action this new belief? What might be the consequences of this action?

3.9.2 – My Take-aways about CONTROL

What are the three biggest insights, learnings and strategies you have taken away from this lesson?

1. _____

_____

2. _____

_____

3. _____

_____

Unit 4

Planning for your best possible self (Commitment to goals and commitment to achievement)

Pi⁺

Unit 4

Purpose of this unit

The purpose of this unit is to explore both goal setting and goal achievement.

Commitment is the extent to which we follow through with our promises — whether this be promises to ourselves or others. In order to do this, we must be able to set goals; but then we need to be able to support this with strategies that move us towards achieving these goals.

People who have a high commitment score will be able to set and achieve goals even if they appear hard. People who have a low commitment score may avoid working towards goals and may even be scared of setting them, for fear of failure.

Lesson 10

Purpose

This session is designed to:

- Introduce the concept of commitment in Mental Toughness

- Prioritise areas of life into workable chunks

- Visualise a picture of your best possible self

- Practice ways to avoid procrastination

4.10.1 — Wheel of School

Below you will see a wheel that has six common areas of school life.

Give each area a score out of 10 for how well you feel this area is working for you at the moment. 10/10 means this area is working really well for you. 1/10 means this area is not working well at all.

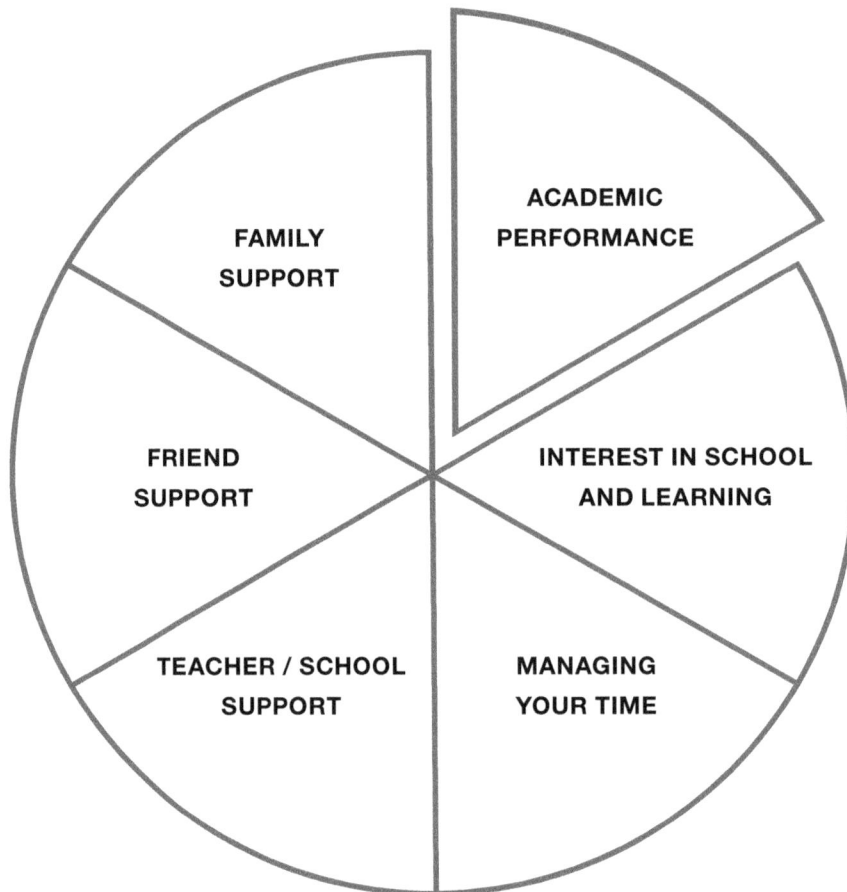

Choose TWO areas and discuss with a partner why you have given them these scores. If possible, provide specific examples.

_____

_____

_____

_____

4.10.2 — Best Possible Self

My chosen area is _____

Looking at your Wheel of School, choose one area that you would like to focus on to improve. Suppose tonight, while you sleep, a miracle occurs. When you awake tomorrow, what will be some of the things you will notice that will tell you this area of your life has suddenly gotten better? What does your day look like, sound like and feel like? Who are you talking to? What are other people saying? What are you doing?

Project yourself forward into the future. Imagine that everything has gone as well as it possibly could. You have worked hard and succeeded at accomplishing the goal you set for this area. Think of this as the realisation that your dreams have come true. Reflect on how well you are utilising your strengths, how you have developed qualities in yourself that you are proud of and how you are living your values on a daily basis. How will you be thinking, feeling and behaving? Visualise yourself satisfied with who you are and how you are living your life. Take some time now to write your story …

4.10.3 — My Take-aways about COMMITMENT

What are the three biggest insights, learnings and strategies you have taken away from this lesson?

1. _____

   _____

2. _____

   _____

3. _____

   _____

Lesson 11

Purpose

This session is designed to:

- Set SMART goals

- Avoid procrastinating and prioritise time

- Plan ways to achieve goals

- Strategise goals with GROW

4.11.1 — SMART Goals

Think about the area of the wheel you have just written a story about and consider how you would like this area to be.

By doing so you will be creating a goal. But not just any goal … a SMART goal. This means your goal is Specific, Measurable, Authentic, Realistic, Time-bound. Have a look at the example below:

SMART area	Question	Response
Specific	What specifically would you like to achieve?	Prepare for my in-class exam, assessment task for English
Measurable	How will you measure the goal or know you have achieved it?	Have written notes that summarise quotes and key themes from the book we are studying
Authentic	How does the goal relate to your interests or strengths?	Share and liaise with friends to discuss and learn in a group — which is my preferred way of learning
Realistic	Is the goal realistic for you but still encourages you to stretch yourself?	It has to be done and it's not something I have done before
Time-bound	When do you need to complete this specific task by?	The task is due on _____ so I would like my full summary completed by _____

Now rewrite your response into one or two sentences to form your SMART Goal.

By the end of _____ I will have some written notes that summarise key themes and quotes from the book we are reading in English. These notes will be based on my own readings and discussions with peers.

Now it's your turn

Think about the area of the wheel you have just written a story about and consider how you would like this area to be. By doing so you will be creating a goal. But not just any goal ... a SMART goal. This means your goal is Specific, Measurable, Authentic, Realistic, Time-bound.

SMART area	Question	Response
Specific	What specifically would you like to achieve?	
Measurable	How will you measure the goal or know you have achieved it?	
Authentic	How does the goal relate to your interests or strengths?	
Realistic	Is the goal realistic for you but still encourages you to stretch yourself?	
Time-bound	When do you need to complete this specific task by?	

My SMART Goal: "By the end of _____ I will have _____ ."

_____

_____

_____

_____

4.11.2 — Mind Mapping SMART Goals

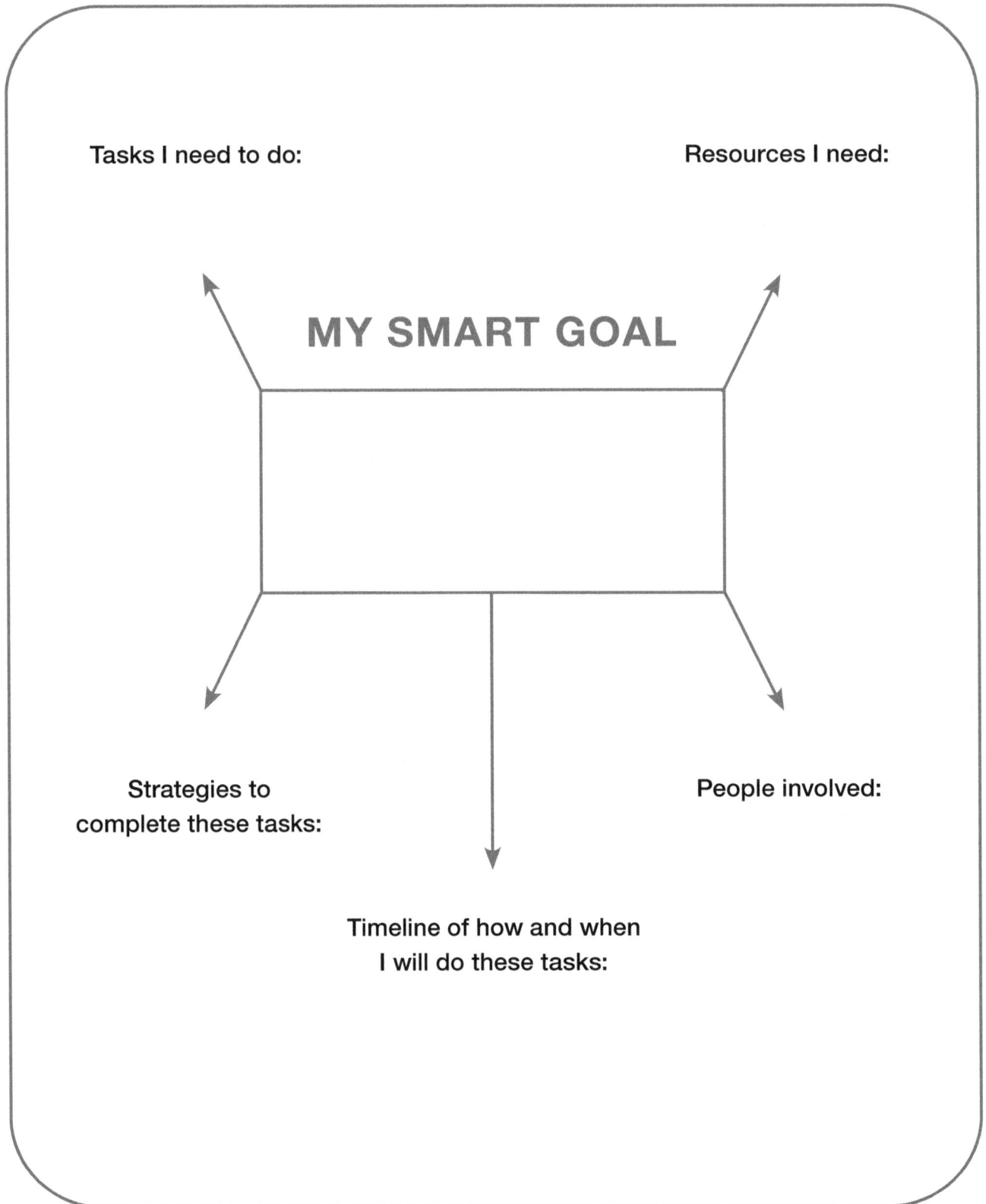

Tasks I need to do:

Resources I need:

MY SMART GOAL

Strategies to
complete these tasks:

People involved:

Timeline of how and when
I will do these tasks:

4.11.3 — The Urgent/Important Matrix

In a speech by President Dwight D. Eisenhower in 1954, he said: "I have two kinds of problems: the urgent and the important. The urgent are not important, and the important are never urgent." This became known as the 'Eisenhower Principle' and is a common method people use to organise their time in order to achieve their goals.

This means the key to being effective is not just being busy, but being busy in the right areas … the areas that will contribute to you achieving your goals. In a nutshell, important activities tend to be those that lead us towards achieving our own goals; whereas urgent activities tend to have timelines placed on us, from other people, that have consequences.

Either way, we need to be careful to not spend too much time doing things that are not important and not urgent — as these become time-wasters and distractions. Instead we need to prioritise those things that are urgent and important.

Sometimes we can get confused between what is urgent and what is important. The Urgent/Important Matrix is a tool that we can use to think about our priorities and how we handle them. Think about the week you have ahead of you and write down all the things you need to do — including commitments with family and friends, school, extra-curricular activities and homework tasks. **For example:**

Urgent — Important	Important — Not Urgent
Assessment deadlines Creating a study timetable	Building friendships at lunch time Going to the gym
Urgent — Not Important	**Not Important — Not Urgent**
Responding to a friend's phone call Checking emails	Checking Facebook Watching Netflix

Now it's your turn

Think about the week you have ahead of you and write down all the things you need to do — including commitments with family and friends, school, extra-curricular activities and homework tasks.

Urgent — Important	Important — Not Urgent
Urgent — Not Important	**Not Important — Not Urgent**

4.11.4 — My Take-aways about COMMITMENT

What are the three biggest insights, learnings and strategies you have taken away from this lesson?

1. _____

_____

2. _____

_____

3. _____

_____

Lesson 12

Purpose

This session is designed to:

- Explore strategies to achieve goals

- Use the GROW model

4.12.1 — Tower Challenge

4.12.2 — GROW Your Goals

The GROW Model of coaching is one of the most popular coaching models used around the world today. It is accredited to Sir John Whitmore (as being the most popular contributor), however no one person is the author of the model. Have a go at using the model and its associated questions to help either yourself or others to gain clarity about an issue or a goal and the associated strategies to achieve the goal.

QUESTIONS	RESPONSE
G — What is the GOAL?	
• What is an urgent and important goal you would like to achieve in the coming weeks or months? • If you were to visualise yourself having completed this goal, what do you see yourself doing or feeling? • When would you like this goal to be achieved by? • How will you know you have achieved your goal? What is the measure? • In one sentence, what is the goal you seek to achieve?	
R — What is your REALITY?	
• What challenges or obstacles might prevent you from moving towards your goal? • Which aspects do you have control or no control over? • Who could you speak to for more support?	

QUESTIONS	RESPONSE
O — What are the OPTIONS?	
• How important is achieving this goal to you? Why? • What if you don't achieve your goal? What is the outcome? • If you spoke to someone who had already achieved this goal, what might they suggest? • If you secretly knew what to do first, what might it be? • If you randomly listed six actions you could do to achieve the goal, what would they be?	
W — Planning a WAY forward?	
• From the actions you have just listed, choose two actions you will commit to. • When will you have done these things by? • When will you start actioning this? • On a scale of 1-10, how committed are you to get this done?	

4.12.3 — My Take-aways about COMMITMENT

What are the three biggest insights, learnings and strategies you have taken away from this lesson?

1. _____

_____

2. _____

_____

3. _____

_____

Unit 5

Developing a Growth Mindset (Challenge with risks and challenges with learning)

Pi⁺

Unit 5

Purpose of this unit

The purpose of this unit is to explore how accepting and moving through challenges can build Mental Toughness.

Challenge is the extent to which you see changes as opportunities and the extent to which you are prepared to seek out challenges by taking risks in learning new concepts.

People who have a high challenge score will be able to commit to others; take part in new projects even if they are not the best at them; enjoy competition; and tend to volunteer more. They tend to take measured risks in the name of improvement.

People who have a low challenge score are more likely to have fixed mindsets and may avoid high pressure situations, preferring to sit out and not participate. They respond poorly in competitions, or when asked to do something they don't enjoy. Sometimes they feel unsupported by others and may be quick to blame others when things go wrong.

Lesson 13

Purpose

This session is designed to:

- Introduce the role challenges play in building our mental toughness

- Identify ways we respond to challenges

- Create challenging experiences so students can reflect on their own responses

- Explore the role that hope plays in managing challenges

5.13.1 — Responding to Challenges

Experiencing challenges is a normal part of life. How we respond to these challenges goes a long way to becoming mentally tough. People can respond in physical ways by throwing things; verbal ways by yelling; social ways by sharing their grievance or ignoring a person. Either way, the most important part of experiencing challenges is learning from them so we can move through them and build our Mental Toughness and resilience to future challenges. For example, the purpose of sitting an exam is to test your understanding of key learning concepts. This can feel quite challenging for some people. As a result, they may cram studying; be really organised and study well in advance; or they may avoid studying altogether. Each decision and response has a consequence. Consider the scenario below and then brainstorm the various ways we can choose to respond.

Challenging situation	Positive Response to challenge	Negative Response to challenge	Bigger Learning or purpose of the challenge
E.g. You are about to sit your yearly Maths exam			
What is another example?			

5.13.2 — Traffic Jam Challenge

Start position

- Divide class into teams of 6-7 students each.

- Groups A and B will perform this task together and groups C and D will be together.

- Group A line up behind each other, next to one of the markers on the floor and face Group B who are also lined up behind each other.

- You will notice there is a free space in the middle between the two teams (see picture below).

Group A								Group B						
v	v	v	v	v	v	v	v	v	v	v	v	v	v	v
1	2	3	4	5	6	7	FS	1	2	3	4	5	6	7

- 'v' indicates a marker on the floor such as a witch's hat or a piece of paper.

- FS indicates a free space in the middle to begin the exercise.

The Challenge

- The aim of the game is for Group A and Group B to swap the positions of all their people so that Group A is standing were Group B was, and vice-versa.

- This means the two sides have to work their way across to the opposite side.

- Both sides must work together or you will end up in a jam and will need to restart the challenge.

Rules of the game

- There is only one free space in the middle of the two teams.

- Students cannot move backwards.

- A person can only move forward to an empty space.

- A person cannot jump over or pass their own team member.

- Only one person may move at a time.

- Only one spot (v) per person is allowed (no sharing).

- If any of these rules are broken, the group must begin again.

5.13.3 — High Hopes

Hope is defined as 'a positive motivational state that is based on an interactively derived sense of successful (a) agency (goal-directed energy) and (b) pathways (planning to meet goals)'. (Snyder, Irving & Anderson, 1991)

In a nutshell, this refers to:

- Having a clear goal that drives us towards possibility
- Acknowledging the multiple pathways we can use to achieve our goal
- Accessing our will or motivation to take action that moves us towards our goal
- Remaining flexible to move around potential blocks or barriers

What are three hopes that you have for the future?

1. _____

_____

2. _____

_____

3. _____

_____

5.13.4 — My Take-aways about CHALLENGE

What are the three biggest insights, learnings and strategies you have taken away from this lesson?

1. _____

_____

2. _____

_____

3. _____

_____

Lesson 14

Purpose

This session is designed to:

- Encourage students to reflect on learning for their own advice

- Explore beliefs, where they come from and how to question them

- Review the concepts of fixed and growth mindsets

- Map the journey of heroes and heroines

5.14.1 — Dear Younger Me

Think about what challenges existed for you when you were in Year 7 at school. What are the three biggest pieces of advice you would give to yourself, given the wisdom and experience you have now?

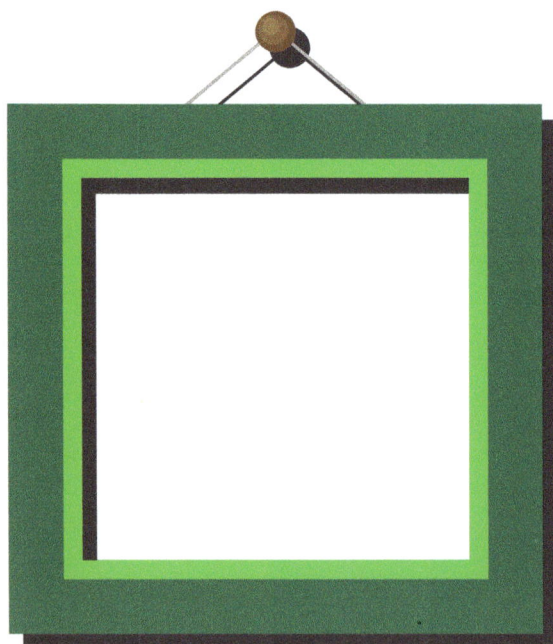

5.14.2 — What is possible?

Which of the following statements are true or false? Explain why to your partner.	True/False
You can't start a business if you're under 16 years of age	
Failing in an exam means failing in life	
Having big dreams is a waste of time and energy	
You can't achieve great grades in school if your parents are uneducated	
You can't play sport if you are overweight	
In order to go on holidays, you have to have money	
You can't learn a new language as an adult	

Discussion Questions

1. What and who shapes our responses?

_____

_____

2. Where do these beliefs come from about what is possible?

_____

_____

3. What possibilities lie ahead for you?

_____

_____

5.14.3 — My Take-aways about CHALLENGE

What are the three biggest insights, learnings and strategies you have taken away from this lesson?

1. _____

   _____

2. _____

   _____

3. _____

   _____

Lesson 15

Purpose

This session is designed to:

- Explore failures, mistakes and challenges we may experience

- Use the 'FAT Formula' (Feel, Act, Think) to reflect on responding to setbacks

5.15.1 — Managing setbacks

We have already discussed the relationship between thoughts, feelings and behaviour. We have also discussed how our beliefs about our ability can be challenged and questioned when choosing a growth mindset. The next step is to use this knowledge to help us better manage any setbacks when they occur. We can do this using the 'FAT Formula' – turning setbacks into opportunities.

F – Feelings   A – Actions   T – Thinking

	THE SETBACK E.g. Struggling to understand the concepts expected in an English assessment task	
NEGATIVE		**POSITIVE**
Thinking option "I can't."		*Thinking option* "It's hard but I can get there."
Action options give up, blame others		*Action options* set small goals, seek support
Feeling options frustrated, nervous, uncertain		*Feeling options* hope, possibility, curiosity
	OPPORTUNITIES Learning from others shows bravery and courage. Persistence breeds stamina and resilience.	

Consider the following scenario and insert how FAT might look with a negative and a positive response.

	THE SETBACK Suzy has set herself a goal of making it to the regional athletics carnival. She has been training hard – but on the day of competition she just didn't perform well and did not make the swim team.	
NEGATIVE		**POSITIVE**
Thinking option		Thinking option
Action options		Action options
Feeling options		Feeling options
	OPPORTUNITIES	

5.15.2 — Predicting setbacks and opportunities

Think about a goal you set, back in Unit 4; and consider any potential setbacks you may encounter. Explore both the positive and negative options available to you. How will you turn any potential setbacks into learning opportunities?

GOAL	POSSIBLE SETBACKS	
NEGATIVE		**POSITIVE**
Thinking option		Thinking option
Action options		Action options
Feeling options		Feeling options
	OPPORTUNITIES	

5.15.3 — My Take-aways about CHALLENGE

What are the three biggest insights, learnings and strategies you have taken away from this lesson?

1. _____

_____

2. _____

_____

3. _____

_____

Unit 6

Creating Positive Relationships (Confidence relationships)

Pi⁺

Unit 6

Purpose of this unit

The purpose of this unit is to explore the role relationships play in supporting the achievement of our goals.

Confidence relationship is the extent to which we are able to express our opinions whilst still respecting the opinions of others.

People who have a high confidence relationship score will be able to stand their ground and be assertive when required.

People who have a low confidence relationship score may avoid speaking up in groups, preferring to stand back; and may avoid opportunities to share insights and opinions. This may hinder goal achievement if they do not ask for support or access opportunities for support by taking risks to grow.

Lesson 16

Purpose

This session is designed to:

- Help students recognise the role trust plays in relationships

- Help students experience vulnerability in safe and positive ways

- Identify how relationships can be an important part of growing

6.16.1 – Gratitude Letter

6.16.2 — My Take-aways about CONFIDENCE

What are the three biggest insights, learnings and strategies you have taken away from this lesson?

1. _____

_____

2. _____

_____

3. _____

_____

Lesson 17

Purpose

This session is designed to:

- Explore the concept of values and where they come from

- Build on students' knowledge of character strengths

- Build students' awareness of the strengths of others

6.17.1 — Lifeboat

You are on a ship in the middle of the ocean and it is sinking. There is one lifeboat left which can only hold six people (you and five others). As the Captain, you have to choose who out of the 10 remaining passengers gets a place on the lifeboat. You have called for help, although the rescue boats will not be able to reach you for at least a week – meaning the people you leave behind may perish.

The list you have is as follows:

1. Sophia is 22 and a cheerleader who was on the boat to relax from her recent breast augmentation surgery. She suffers from clinical depression and is on medication as a result.

2. Anne is 41, a social worker and single mother with two school-aged children at home. She is also obese and often seen over-eating when on the ship.

3. Sam is 15, on probation for stealing money from a local shop. He is charming, friendly and helpful; although not trustworthy.

4. Dr Kane is 52, in good health; but has only one arm from a childhood accident. He is very knowledgeable but has a tendency to talk a lot and tell others how to do things.

5. Mustafa is 24 and a fitness instructor with an athletic build; however he has HIV from a blood transfusion he received when he was a child.

6. Chris is 45 and currently unemployed but he used to work on both big ships and small ones. He is comfortable on the ocean but his alcoholism resulted in him losing his job.

7. Shakira is 18 and pregnant. She is no longer with the father and doesn't seem to worry about planning for the future for herself and her baby.

8. Toni is 22 and just dropped out of university to pursue her acting dream. She looks to God to help guide her path.

9. Taylor is 35, a nurse with four young children. She's a chronic smoker.

10. Chen is 26, an IT specialist who is on a student visa from Malaysia … and you think he may be on the autism spectrum.

Who will you take on the boat and why?

6.17.2 — Reflecting on strengths

Our character strengths are strongly linked to our values. This means when something is important to us (a value), we will behave in ways that reflect this (our character). Values are something that's important to us. If something is important we tend to prioritise it – which drives our decisions and our actions. If we become obsessive about a value, we can overplay our strengths and this can have negative ramifications in relationships.

My top five signature strengths	How I use this strength	The value that relates to this strength	Why is this important to me?
E.g. Leadership	I like helping people with decision making	Getting things done	When I make decisions, I feel like I am in control and I am able to achieve things

6.17.3 — Strengths Class Map

Character Strengths	Student Names
Creativity	
Curiosity	
Judgement	
Love of Learning	
Perspective	
Bravery	
Perseverance	
Honesty	
Zest	
Love	
Kindness	
Social Intelligence	
Teamwork	
Fairness	
Leadership	
Forgiveness	
Humility	
Self-Regulation	
Appreciation of Beauty and Excellence	
Gratitude	
Hope	
Humour	
Spirituality	

6.17.4 — Character Strengths Classification

CHARACTER STRENGTHS

- **Creativity** – Thinking of novel and productive ways to conceptualise and do things.

- **Curiosity** – Taking an interest in ongoing experience for its own sake; exploring and discovering.

- **Judgement** – Thinking things through and examining them from all sides; not jumping to conclusions; being able to change one's mind in light of evidence; weighing all evidence fairly.

- **Love of Learning** – Mastering new skills, topics, and bodies of knowledge, whether on one's own or formally; going beyond curiosity to describe the tendency to add systematically to what one knows.

- **Perspective** – Being able to provide wise counsel to others; having ways of looking at the world that make sense to oneself and to other people.

- **Bravery** – Not shrinking from threat, challenge, difficulty, or pain; speaking up for what is right even if there is opposition; acting on convictions even if unpopular.

- **Perseverance** – Finishing what one starts; persisting in a course of action in spite of obstacles; taking pleasure in completing tasks.

- **Honesty** – Speaking the truth but more broadly presenting oneself in a genuine way and acting in a sincere way; being without pretence; taking responsibility for one's feelings and actions.

- **Zest** – Approaching life with excitement and energy; not doing things halfway or half-heartedly; living life as an adventure; feeling alive and activated.

- **Love** – Valuing close relationships with others, in particular those in which sharing and caring are reciprocated; being close to people.

- **Kindness** – Doing favours and good deeds for others; helping them; taking care of them.

- **Social Intelligence** – Being aware of the motives and feelings of other people and oneself; knowing what to do to fit into different social situations; knowing what makes other people tick.

- **Teamwork** – Working well as a member of a group or team; being loyal to the group; doing one's share.

- **Fairness** – Treating all people the same according to notions of fairness and justice; not letting personal feelings bias decisions about others; giving everyone a fair chance.

- **Leadership** – Encouraging a group of which one is a member to get things done, and at the same time maintaining good relations within the group; organising group activities and seeing that they happen.

- **Forgiveness** – Forgiving those who have done wrong; accepting the shortcomings of others; giving people a second chance; not being vengeful.

- **Humility** – Letting one's accomplishments speak for themselves; not regarding oneself as more special than one is.

- **Prudence** – Being careful about one's choices; not taking undue risks; not saying or doing things that might later be regretted.

- **Self-Regulation** – Regulating what one feels and does; being disciplined; controlling one's appetites and emotions.

- **Appreciation of Beauty and Excellence** – Noticing and appreciating beauty, excellence, and/or skilled performance in various domains of life, from nature to art to mathematics to science to everyday experiences.

- **Gratitude** – Being aware of and thankful for the good things that happen; taking time to express thanks.

- **Hope** – Expecting the best in the future and working to achieve it; believing that a good future is something that can be brought about.

- **Humour** – Liking to laugh and tease; bringing smiles to other people; seeing the light side; making (not necessarily telling) jokes.

- **Spirituality** – Having coherent beliefs about the higher purpose and meaning of the universe; knowing where one fits within the larger scheme; having beliefs about the meaning of life that shape conduct and provide comfort.

Source: http://www.viacharacter.org/viainstitute/classification.aspx

6.17.5 — My Take-aways about CONFIDENCE

What are the three biggest insights, learnings and strategies you have taken away from this lesson?

1. _____

_____

2. _____

_____

3. _____

_____

Lesson 18

Purpose

This session is designed to:

- Help students identify healthy ways of communicating in times of stress or pressure

- Encourage students to take responsibility for their actions and responses to others in times of stress or pressure using the principle of Above and Below the Line

- Practice giving clear and effective communication whilst identifying barriers

6.18.1 — Above and Below the Line

Look at the list of comments that were made in the previous activity and categorise them into those which were 'Above the Line' and those which were 'Below the Line'.

When we choose to take responsibility for the things we can control, that contribute to our success or failure, we are acting 'Above the Line'. However, when we choose to blame others or our circumstances, we are seen to be acting 'Below the Line'.

SITUATION 1 **Partner activities**	**RESPONDING ABOVE THE LINE**	EXAMPLE: **Ownership** **Accountability** **Responsibility**
	RESPONDING BELOW THE LINE	EXAMPLE: **Blame** **Excuses** **Denial**

SITUATION 2 **You have just received your marks for an exam or an assessment task**	**RESPONDING ABOVE THE LINE**	EXAMPLE: **Ownership** **Accountability** **Responsibility**
	RESPONDING BELOW THE LINE	EXAMPLE: **Blame** **Excuses** **Denial**

6.18.2 — My Take-aways about CONFIDENCE

What are the three biggest insights, learnings and strategies you have taken away from this lesson?

1. _____

_____

2. _____

_____

3. _____

_____

Unit 7

Be Your Own Coach
(Confidence abilities)

Pi⁺

Unit 7

Purpose of this unit

The purpose of this unit is to explore the importance of having confidence in our personal abilities as well as how we interact with others.

Confidence is the extent to which we believe we are capable of achieving and completing tasks as well as standing our ground and being assertive when required.

People who have a high confidence score will be able to set and achieve goals even if they appear hard. People who have a low confidence score may avoid working towards goals and may even be scared of setting them … for fear of failure.

Lesson 19

Purpose

This session is designed to:

- Identify the link between goals, communication and confidence

- Encourage students to identify how confidence grows from applying effort, taking measured risks and reflecting on progress

7.19.1 — My Take-aways about CONFIDENCE

What are the three biggest insights, learnings and strategies you have taken away from this lesson?

1. _____

_____

2. _____

_____

3. _____

_____

Lesson 20

Purpose

This session is designed to:

- Highlight the effort required when listening to others

- Review the concept of Mental Toughness and the 4Cs

- Establish mental cues with related strategies so students can draw on these in the future

7.20.1 — Measuring Mental Toughness

Understanding the 4Cs	Self-rating scale: Circle where you currently lie
Control (Life) The Control-life scale refers to how much control you believe you have in your life. Do you believe you have complete control over everything in your life (10/10), or do you believe you are at the mercy of everything around you **(1/10)?**	1 2 3 4 5 6 7 8 9 10
Control (Emotions) The Control-emotions scale refers to how well you are able to manage your emotions. Are you able to completely control your emotions to a point of shutting off (10/10), or do your emotions control you to a point where you find it difficult to function **(1/10)?**	1 2 3 4 5 6 7 8 9 10
Commitment (Setting Goals) This Commitment scale refers to how often and how well you set goals for yourself. Do you set goals, create a vision or set an intention for how you want learning or tasks to be (10/10), or do you let others tell you what to do and how you should be when it comes to learning and achieving **(1/10)?**	1 2 3 4 5 6 7 8 9 10
Commitment (Achieving Goals) This Commitment scale refers to the way in which you work towards your goals and targets. Do you keep the promises you make to yourself and others when it comes to achieving tasks or goals (10/10), or do you often make promises to yourself and others and not follow through or achieve them **(1/10)?**	1 2 3 4 5 6 7 8 9 10
Challenge (Take on Challenges) This Challenge scale refers to how you see new opportunities, challenges and change. Do you seek out and embrace challenges as opportunities for growth and learning (10/10), or do you avoid challenges, preferring to stay inside your comfort zone **(1/10)?**	1 2 3 4 5 6 7 8 9 10
Challenge (Overcome Challenges) This Challenge scale refers to how you overcome challenges and change. Do you reflect on mistakes or failures as opportunities for growth and learning and try again (10/10), or do you reflect on mistakes and failures as 'just the way it is' and accept the result **(1/10)?**	1 2 3 4 5 6 7 8 9 10

Understanding the 4Cs	Self-rating scale: Circle where you currently lie
Confidence (Abilities) The Confidence-abilities scale refers to your awareness and use of your strengths. Do you confidently know and use your strengths when needed (10/10), or are you uncertain about your strengths and your own abilities when it comes to learning **(1/10)?**	1 2 3 4 5 6 7 8 9 10
Confidence (Relationships) The Confidence-relationships scale refers to how assertive, reliable and supportive you are in relationships. Do you stand your ground in a respectful manner when you expressing your point or view (10/10), or do you become intimidated and easily led by others' opinions, preferring to hide in the background **(1/10)?**	1 2 3 4 5 6 7 8 9 10

Discuss with a partner why you chose the scores you did ...

7.20.2 — My Take-aways about CONFIDENCE

What are the three biggest insights, learnings and strategies you have taken away from this lesson?

1. _____

_____

2. _____

_____

3. _____

_____

Lesson 21

Purpose

This session is designed to:

- Recap the 4Cs and the related strategies explored in the program

- Explore ways students can maintain positive practice that supports Mental Toughness

- Create a plan that incorporates the principles of Mental Toughness for future goals

7.21.1 — My Mental Toughness Plan

Area of Mental Toughness	Sub-Categories	Question	Tool and Strategy to use
CONTROL	Life Control	In which areas do you have control?	
	Emotional Control	How will you track your emotions and manage these?	
COMMITMENT	Goal Setting	What is it you are trying to achieve? What is your end goal?	
	Goal Striving	What actions are required to move you towards this goal?	
CHALLENGES	Stretching Yourself	How is this goal stretching you to grow?	
	Learning from Experience	What have you done in the past that is similar, that may help you achieve this in the future?	
CONFIDENCE	Confidence in Abilities	What skills or strengths do you have that support you achieving this goal?	
	Interpersonal Confidence	What support do you need from others? Who could you approach and how could you access this support?	

7.21.2 — GROWing my Goal

	Question	Response
GOAL	What is your goal?	
REALITY	What is happening now?	
OPTIONS	What options do you have for moving you towards this goal?	
WAY FORWARD	Considering these options, what actions will you take and by when?	

In Closing

Program
Feedback

Pi⁺

Congratulations, You Made It To The End. Well Done!

Program Feedback

Thank you for participating in this program. We hope you have enjoyed it and will take away some new tools to help you grow in Mental Toughness. We too continue to grow in Mental Toughness and welcome your feedback about the program. Please share your thoughts with us below.

Read the following statements and rate on a scale of 1-5	1 = Poor, 2 = Weak, 3 = OK, 4 = Good, 5 = Excellent
1. I found the activities …	1 2 3 4 5
2. I found the content to be …	1 2 3 4 5
3. I now have more skills to cope with stress …	1 2 3 4 5
4. I am able to better support myself and others	1 2 3 4 5
5. I found this program helpful and useful	1 2 3 4 5

Please send any other feedback through to info@thepositivityinstitute.com.au.

6. Overall, what did you enjoy most about this program?

_____

_____

_____

7. What was your biggest learning throughout the program?

_____

_____

_____

8. Overall, what could make this program even better?

_____

_____

_____

THANK YOU

☺

The Positivity Institute

www.ingramcontent.com/pod-product-compliance
Lightning Source LLC
Chambersburg PA
CBHW060957030426
42334CB00032B/3270